Understanding the
U.S. Constitution

Sally Senzell Isaacs

Crabtree Publishing Company

www.crabtreebooks.com

Author: Sally Senzell Isaacs
Editor-in-Chief: Lionel Bender
Editor: Kelley MacAulay
Proofreaders: Adrianna Morganelli,
    Crystal Sikkens
Project editor: Robert Walker
Photo research: Susannah Jayes
Designer: Malcolm Smythe
Production coordinator: Katherine Berti
Production: Kim Richardson
Prepress technician: Margaret Amy Salter
Consultant: Professor Richard Jensen,
    history teacher, consultant, and author

This book was produced for
    Crabtree Publishing Company
    by Bender Richardson White, U.K.

Cover:
A replication of the actual United States Constitution
with the American flag
Title page:
A parade in New York to honor Alexander Hamilton
and the new U.S. Constitution
Photographs:
© Art Archive: Library of Congress: p. 7
© Corbis: Bettmann: p. 17; Steve Chenn: p. 23; Lester Lefkowitz:
    p. 15 (bottom left); Gregg Newton: p. 4
© Library of Congress: p. 12 (cph 3a53278), 14 (cph 3g02108),
    29 (cph 3g02399—top right)
© Northwind Picture Archives: p. 1, 5, 6, 8, 9 (bottom right),
    10, 11, 13, 16, 18, 19, 21, 24
© Shutterstock.com: cover, p. 15 (top right), 20, 22, 25, 26, 27,
    28, 29 (bottom right)
© The Granger Collection: p. 9 (top right)

Library and Archives Canada Cataloguing in Publication

Isaacs, Sally Senzell, 1950-
    Understanding the US Constitution / Sally Senzell Isaacs.

(Documenting early America)
Includes index.
ISBN 978-0-7787-4373-6 (bound).--ISBN 978-0-7787-4378-1 (pbk.)

    1. United States. Constitution--Juvenile literature. 2. Constitutional
history--United States--Juvenile literature. 3. United States--Politics
and government--1775-1783--Juvenile literature. 4. United States--
Politics and government--1783-1789--Juvenile literature. I. Title.
II. Series: Isaacs, Sally Senzell, 1950- . Documenting early America.

E303.I83 2008   j342.7302'9   C2008-905555-1

Library of Congress Cataloging-in-Publication Data

Isaacs, Sally Senzell, 1950-
    Understanding the U.S. Constitution / Sally Senzell Isaacs.
        p. cm. -- (Documenting early America)
    Includes index.
    ISBN-13: 978-0-7787-4378-1 (pbk. : alk. paper)
    ISBN-10: 0-7787-4378-0 (pbk. : alk. paper)
    ISBN-13: 978-0-7787-4373-6 (reinforced library binding : alk. paper)
    ISBN-10: 0-7787-4373-X (reinforced library binding : alk. paper)
    1. United States. Constitution--Juvenile literature. 2. Constitutional
history--United States--Juvenile literature. 3. United States--Politics and
government--1775-1783--Juvenile literature. 4. United States--Politics
and government--1783-1789--Juvenile literature. I. Title.

    E303.I83 2009
    320.973--dc22

                                        2008036601

Crabtree Publishing Company

www.crabtreebooks.com   1-800-387-7650

Printed in the USA/062011/SN20110520

Published in Canada
Crabtree Publishing
616 Welland Ave.
St. Catharines, Ontario
L2M 5V6

Published in the United States
Crabtree Publishing
PMB 59051
350 Fifth Ave., 59th Floor
New York, NY 10118

Published in the United Kingdom
Crabtree Publishing
Maritime House
Basin Road North, Hove
BN41 1WR

Published in Australia
Crabtree Publishing
3 Charles Street
Coburg North
VIC, 3058

Contents

The Constitution

In 1787, more than 220 years ago, the leaders of the United States wrote the **Constitution**. The Constitution is a plan or set of rules that the **national government** follows. It explains how laws are made, how leaders are chosen, and what the government can and cannot do.

The Constitution was not easy to write. The leaders had to make many decisions. Who would make the laws? Who could become **president**? What would happen if people wanted to change the Constitution?

▶ *Today, visitors can see the Constitution at the National Archives building in Washington, D.C.*

Different states

At the time, there were 13 states in the nation. Some states had many people. Some had few people. The people in different states lived in different ways and cared about different things. Each state wanted to be treated fairly. The leaders **debated** many issues before they finished writing the Constitution. This powerful document still guides the United States government today.

▼ *In the beginning, the United States consisted of 13 states.*

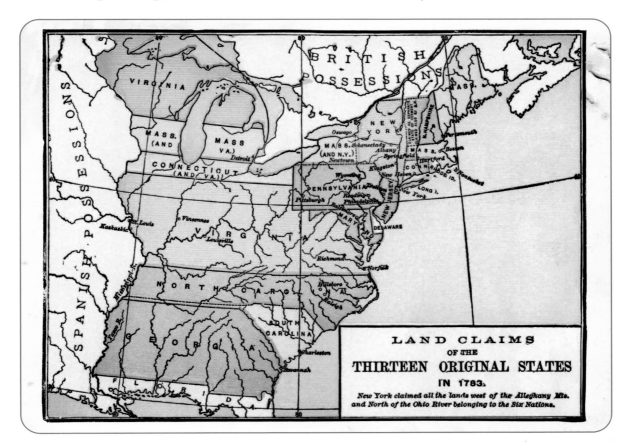

Fighting for Freedom

Before the United States became a nation, there were 13 **colonies.** A colony is a place where people live that is far from the country that rules it. The 13 colonies belonged to Britain, which was about 3,000 miles away. People in the colonies had to follow Britain's laws and pay **taxes** to Britain. A tax is money that is used to run a country. In the 1760s, Britain needed more money to fight a war with France. British lawmakers made the colonists pay more taxes every time they bought such items as newspapers, sugar, tea, or cloth.

◄ *Colonists— people who lived in the colonies— held meetings to discuss ways of protesting against Britain's taxes.*

▲ *George Washington, seen here on the white horse, became the general of the American army during the Revolution.*

America and Britain go to war

The colonists started to talk about independence from Britain. They wanted to be free to rule their own country and make their own laws. In 1775, Britain's King George III sent soldiers and officials to make the colonists pay their taxes. Colonial soldiers, led by George Washington from Virginia, lined up to fight for their freedom. They fought a long six-year war. It was called the **American Revolution** or Revolutionary War. A revolution is a strong action by people to change their government.

A New Nation

While soldiers fought the war, leaders from each colony met in Philadelphia, Pennsylvania. This group was called the **Continental Congress.** In July 1776, members of the Congress wrote and signed the **Declaration of Independence.** This document told King George III—and the world—that the colonies were becoming a new nation. It would be called the United States of America.

▼ *In July 1776, the Continental Congress wrote the Declaration of Independence.*

The first united states

After the Declaration was signed, the 13 colonies became the first 13 states. Each state formed its own government. People in each state chose leaders to make laws for their state.

The states also wanted to join together to form a national government. This government would make laws for the new nation. Congress wrote a plan for the government called the **Articles of Confederation**.

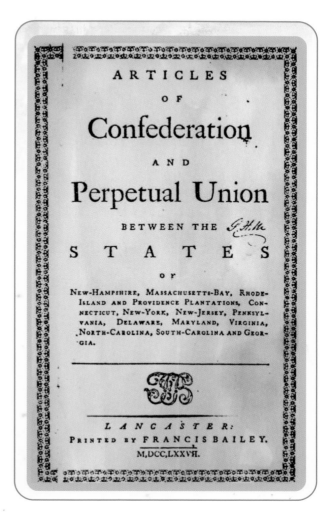

▲ *The Articles of Confederation*

▶ *The Articles were printed in newspapers for everyone in the country to read.*

The Articles Fail

In 1781, Congress and the states agreed to the Articles of Confederation. This was the first national government of the United States. There was no president of the nation; Congress ran the government. **Representatives** from each state came to Congress to speak for the people of that state. However, there were problems with the government. Under the Articles, the national government was too weak and the states were too powerful.

◄ *Congress met at the Pennsylvania State House in Philadelphia. The Declaration of Independence had been signed here in 1776.*

A lack of money

The government owed a lot of money. It owed money to the soldiers who fought in the American Revolution. It owed money to other countries. The national government had no power to tax people. It could only ask the states for money. Sometimes, the states refused to give any money to the government.

Shays's Rebellion

The state governments were short of money, too. When they raised taxes, people grew angry. In Massachusetts, poor farmers, led by Daniel Shays, attacked government buildings. The national government did not have enough money or soldiers to help the state troops, who eventually stopped the attacks.

◄ Daniel Shays led angry farmers to a Massachusetts courthouse.

Starting Over

Would the United States fall apart? The states acted like 13 separate countries. They passed their own laws. They printed their own money. Some states taxed one another for goods that came across their borders. Arguments broke out between states. The national government did not have the power to solve these problems.

▲ *James Madison is sometimes called the "Father of the Constitution." He helped develop many of the ideas.*

On May 25, 1787, representatives from the states met in Philadelphia. They met to fix the Articles of Confederation. Before long, they decided to write a new plan for the government. This plan became known as the United States Constitution.

An important meeting

Starting over was a big step! The representatives, called **delegates**, were ready for the job. Most of the delegates were well-known leaders in their states. George Washington, Benjamin Franklin, Alexander Hamilton, and James Madison were the most famous delegates. The meeting to write the new government plan was called the Constitutional **Convention.**

▼ *The delegates chose George Washington—here in the center of the picture—to be president (leader) of the Constitutional Convention.*

Separating Power

The delegates quickly agreed to a new kind of national government. They did not want one person or group to have too much power. However, they would elect a president. They made three branches, or sections, of government. Each branch handled different jobs. This plan is still used today.

The legislative branch is called Congress. It makes the laws. Congress is divided into two houses, or groups. One house is called the House of Representatives. The other house is called the Senate. States send representatives to both houses.

▶ *This is a design for the Great Seal of the United States, which was made at around the same time as the Constitution was written.*

The laws in action

The executive branch is led by the president. It ensures that the laws are carried out. The president also controls the army and navy, and makes agreements with other countries. The judicial branch is made of courts and judges. They interpret, or explain, the laws. The courts make sure the president and Congress do not overstep their powers.

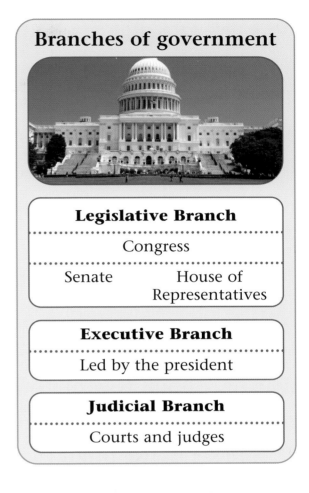

Branches of government

Legislative Branch
Congress

Senate	House of Representatives

Executive Branch
Led by the president

Judicial Branch
Courts and judges

◄ *The delegates met in this room to write the Constitution. The Declaration of Independence was signed in this same room. People can visit the room today.*

Reaching Agreement

The delegates met at the Constitutional Convention from May to September, 1787. Although the summer days were hot, the delegates kept the meeting room windows and doors closed. They did not want anyone to hear their debates and interrupt them. They had important decisions to make, and they did not agree on many issues.

First the delegates debated about how many representatives each state should send to Congress. James Madison explained the Virginia Plan. This plan gave bigger states more representatives. Delegates from smaller states did not think this was fair. They did not want big states to overpower them.

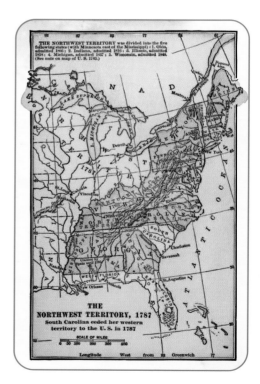

▲ *By 1787, western land, called the Northwest Territory, became part of the United States.*

All states agree at last

Next, William Paterson explained the New Jersey Plan. It gave all states the same number of representatives. After long debates, they found a solution that worked for both sides. It was called the Great Compromise. Under this plan, every state sends two representatives to the Senate. For the House of Representatives, states with more people send more representatives than do states with fewer people.

▼ *Today, each state still sends two representatives to the Senate.*

The Slavery Question

In the Constitution, it says that a state can send one representative to the House of Representatives for every 30,000 people in the state. In southern states, many people owned **slaves**. There were few slaves in northern states. The delegates had to debate whether slaves would be counted in a state's total number of people. If so, states with many slaves would have more representatives.

Slaves

Slave traders captured people in Africa and shipped them to America to work for no pay. The slaves were poorly fed and housed in wooden cabins. They had no rights.

▶ *This is an ad to sell slaves.*

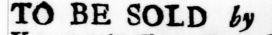

▶ *Slaves worked on large farms. They picked cotton and other crops.*

Not counted in the same way

There were more than 290,000 slaves in Virginia. Three other southern states each had more than 100,000 slaves. Southern delegates wanted slaves to be counted toward representation. Northern delegates voted against this. The delegates compromised again. They decided that every five slaves in a state would be counted as only three people. There were other debates about slavery. Leaders from northern states wanted to end slavery, southern-state leaders did not. The delegates decided that in 21 years (1808), people would no longer be able to bring slaves into the United States.

Debates in the States

Finally on September 15, 1787, 39 delegates at the Convention voted to accept the Constitution. Next, the state governments had to approve it. If nine of the 13 states approved it, the Constitution would **officially** take the place of the Articles of Confederation.

Leaders gathered at state conventions to decide whether to accept the Constitution. People who wanted to accept the Constitution were called Federalists. People who did not want to accept it were called Anti-Federalists.

► *The Constitution document*

It's official

Anti-Federalists were afraid that, under the Constitution, the national government had too much power. After all, they had fought a war against the British to be free to make their own decisions and laws. On December 7, 1787, Delaware became the first state to approve the Constitution. On June 21, 1788, New Hampshire became the ninth state to approve it. The Constitution of the United States was officially accepted!

▼ *A "Ship of State" was paraded on Wall Street, in New York City, in 1788, to honor Alexander Hamilton and the new United States Constitution.*

The Bill of Rights

All 13 states voted "yes" to the Constitution, but many of them asked for something in return. They wanted to add a **Bill of Rights**. A Bill of Rights gives people some protection from the government. It says that people will always have freedom of religion, freedom of speech, fair trials, and other rights.

▼ *The First Amendment promises that the government will not stop people from demonstrating for or saying what they believe.*

▲ *The Sixth and Seventh Amendments promise a fair trial by jury.*

Amendments to the Constitution

Those people who demanded the Bill of Rights wanted to ensure that the government could never take away people's rights. They remembered that British soldiers had arrested colonists who complained about their government. They also remembered that some colonists had been punished for their religious beliefs. James Madison wrote the Bill of Rights as ten **amendments**, or additions, to the Constitution. The amendments were approved first by Congress and then, in 1791, by the state governments and became part of the Constitution.

The New Government

The United States Constitution is one of the most successful government plans in the world. The national government and the state governments have different powers in the country. The national government is the highest; state laws cannot go against national laws. Although no one person makes the laws, the president ensures that they are carried out.

The President's Promise
Each new president says the same oath, or makes a promise, before beginning the job. The president promises to *"preserve, protect, and defend the Constitution of the United States."*

▶ *George Washington said the oath when he was elected as the first U.S. president in 1789.*

Working together

The Constitution also set up **checks and balances** for the three branches of government. With checks and balances, each branch has a say about things that are done by the other branches. For example, Congress—in the legislative branch—can pass a law. However, the president—in the executive branch—can stop, or **veto**, the law if he or she does not agree with it. Also, federal judges—in the judicial branch—can stop a law by saying that it goes against the Constitution.

▼ *The Senate and the House of Representatives meet in the U.S. Capitol Building in Washington, D.C.*

The People Choose

Americans choose their president and their Congress representatives. It is written in the Constitution which people may have these jobs and for how long. For example, Americans elect a president every four years. A president must be someone who was born in the United States and is at least 35 years old. After the four-year term, a president can be re-elected to serve only one more time.

▼ *The U.S. president works with his or her officials and lives in the White House in Washington, D.C.*

Congress and the Supreme Court

Members of the House of Representatives serve for two years. They can be re-elected. Senators serve for six years. They can also be re-elected.

The Supreme Court is the most important court in the nation. Its judges are not elected. Supreme court judges are chosen by the president and then approved by the Senate. They may serve for the rest of their lives.

▼ *The Supreme Court meets in this building in Washington D.C.*

Planning for Change

After the Constitution was written, the population, or total number of people, in the United States kept growing. More and more people moved into the open land west of the 13 states. The leaders who wrote the Constitution had prepared for this! They had included a section explaining how to add new states to the country. Today, the United States has 50 states that reach all the way to the Pacific Ocean.

The Constitution also includes a plan explaining how people can change parts of the Constitution. Amendments can be added, but this is not easy. First, both houses of Congress must pass the amendment. Then three-fourths of the states must approve it.

▲ *In 1971, the 26th Amendment lowered the age at which Americans can vote for a president from 21 years to 18.*

▲ *The Fifteenth Amendment was added in 1870. This amendment gave African Americans the right to vote.*

Standing the test of time

Today, Americans still follow the plans in the U.S. Constitution and the Bill of Rights. These successful plans have now helped shape the country for more than 220 years.

▼ *Today's national flag, the Stars and Stripes*

Timeline

1760 Britain passes new taxes for colonists

1775 First shots of the American Revolution are fired

1776 The Continental Congress signs the Declaration of Independence

1777 Congress agrees to the words of the Articles of Confederation

1781 The Articles of Confederation officially become the first plan of the national government

1783 The American Revolution ends, two years after the last battle

1786 Shays's Rebellion begins in Massachusetts

1787 The Constitutional Convention meets to revise the Articles of Confederation. A new Constitution is written

1788 The Constitution becomes official after nine states accept it

1791 The Bill of Rights becomes part of the Constitution

Websites

1. Ben's Guide to U.S. Government for Kids
http://bensguide.gpo.gov/3-5/documents/constitution/index.html
This site provides information about the Constitution and early American history,
and links to websites where you can read the Constitution in English and Spanish.

2. The National Constitution Center
http://www.constitutioncenter.org/ncc_home_Landing.aspx
Here you can enjoy an interactive experience learning about the Constitution,
as well as the National Constitution Center.

3. The White House for Kids
http://www.whitehouse.gov/kids/constitution/
On this site you will find facts about the Constitution and its amendments, a video
of Constitution Day at the Vice-President's house, and quizzes and word games.

4. Congress for Kids
http://www.congressforkids.net/Constitution_index.htm
This site contains a history of the Constitution and how it was written,
plus fact sheets, quizzes, games, and links to related sites.

5. Social Studies for Kids
http://www.socialstudiesforkids.com/subjects/constitution.htm
Here you will find information about the Constitutional Congress, plus the complete text
of the Constitution, biographies of all the signers, fascinating Constitution facts, and a
comparison of the Articles of Confederation and the Constitution.

6. National Archives and Records Administration
http://www.archives.gov/exhibits/charters/constitution.html
This site includes a transcript of the Constitution of the United States, an image of the
original document, and links to other sites of interest.

Further Reading

Fradin, Dennis Bridnell. *The U.S. Constitution*. Tarrytown, N.Y.: Marshall Cavendish, 2008.

Isaacs, Sally Senzell. *America in the Time of George Washington*.
   Chicago: Heinemann, 1999.

Levy, Elizabeth. *If You Were There When They Signed the Constitution*.
   New York: Scholastic, 1992.

Price, Sean. *Designing America: The Constitutional Convention*.
   Chicago: Raintree, 2008.

Sobel, Syl. *The U.S. Constitution and You*. Hauppauge, N.Y.: Barron's, 2001.

Taylor-Butler, Christine. *The Constitution of the United States*.
   New York: Scholastic, 2008.

Teitelbaum, Michael. *The U.S. Constitution*. Mankato, Minn.: Child's World, 2004.

Glossary

amendment An addition or change to a document

American Revolution The war of independence from Britain

Articles of Confederation The first plans for the national government

Bill of Rights The first ten amendments to the U.S. Constitution

checks and balances In the U.S. government, each branch has a say in the other branches

colony A place where people live that is far from the country that rules it

Constitution A set of plans or rules followed by the national government

convention A meeting

Continental Congress A meeting of state representatives to discuss a subject or make laws

debate To talk about both sides of an issue

Declaration of Independence A document claiming the right of Americans to make their own decisions and laws

delegate A person who speaks for many people at a meeting; a representative

national government The government in charge of an entire country or nation

official Something that is approved

president The leader of the executive branch of national government

representative Someone who speaks for many people when laws are made

slave A person who is owned by another person and usually must work for that person for no pay

tax Money collected from people and businesses for running the government

veto The president's power to stop a new law

Index